How do they make Costumes?

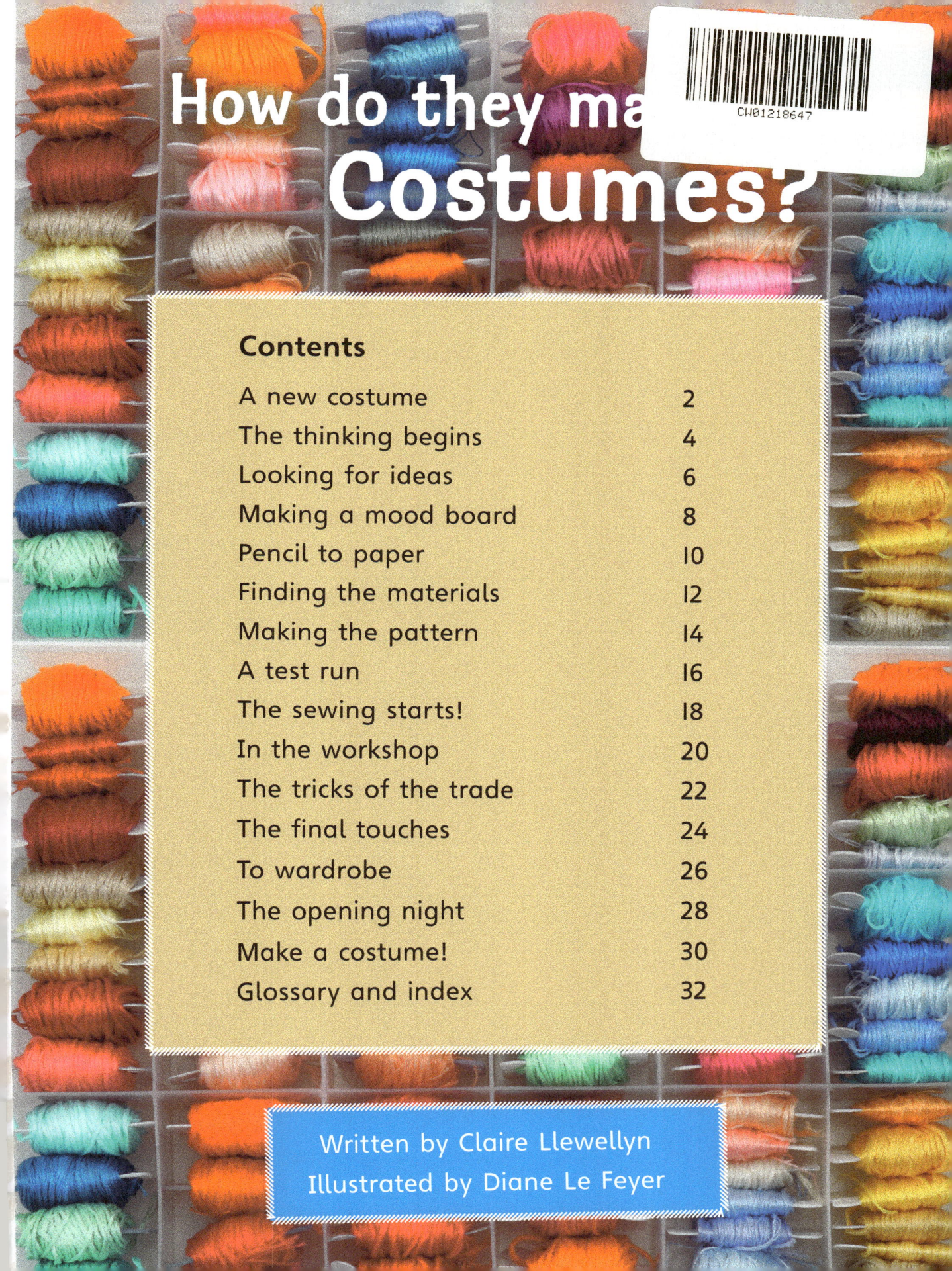

Contents

A new costume	2
The thinking begins	4
Looking for ideas	6
Making a mood board	8
Pencil to paper	10
Finding the materials	12
Making the pattern	14
A test run	16
The sewing starts!	18
In the workshop	20
The tricks of the trade	22
The final touches	24
To wardrobe	26
The opening night	28
Make a costume!	30
Glossary and index	32

Written by Claire Llewellyn
Illustrated by Diane Le Feyer

A new costume

Costumes matter

Costumes are the clothes worn by actors. They play an important part in any film, play or TV programme. Good costumes can help you to understand the story. They also tell you a lot about the characters. Have you ever wondered how costumes are made? They take a lot of planning and many people have to work together to get them just right.

Boots, hats, gloves and belts are all part of an actor's costume.

Did you know?

It's expensive to make new costumes. It's cheaper to hire costumes or buy them in shops.

First steps

When a new play is planned, a **director** is put in charge. The director chooses a costume designer and they meet to talk about the costumes for the play. The director gives the designer a copy of the **script**. Reading the script helps the designer to understand the story and the characters.

Think about it!

Before you start to make a costume, you need to ask two questions:
- How much time is there to make the costume?
- How much money can I spend?

Can you think of anything else you would need to know?

Fancy dress shops hire out costumes, but you can't alter them to fit.

Learning about the play

The thinking begins

Scenes and characters

The costume designer's first task is to look at the different **scenes** in the script. The designer thinks about each character in turn, and asks a lot of questions, such as:

- When and where does this character live?
- How old is this character?
- Is he or she rich or poor?
- What is his or her job?
- Does he or she have to run around in the costume?

Answers to questions like these will help the designer to decide what characters should wear in each scene.

The costume designer

"I've always been very interested in fashion, and I started drawing when I was about five. At college, I studied fashion design. When we learned about the history of costume, I knew I wanted to make costumes for the stage. I enjoy my work: doing research, using my imagination, sewing, and managing a team. It's fun — and very hard work!"

Did you know?

Costume designers usually work with real actors, but they also design costumes for puppet shows and the characters in animated films.

Learning about the play

Looking for ideas

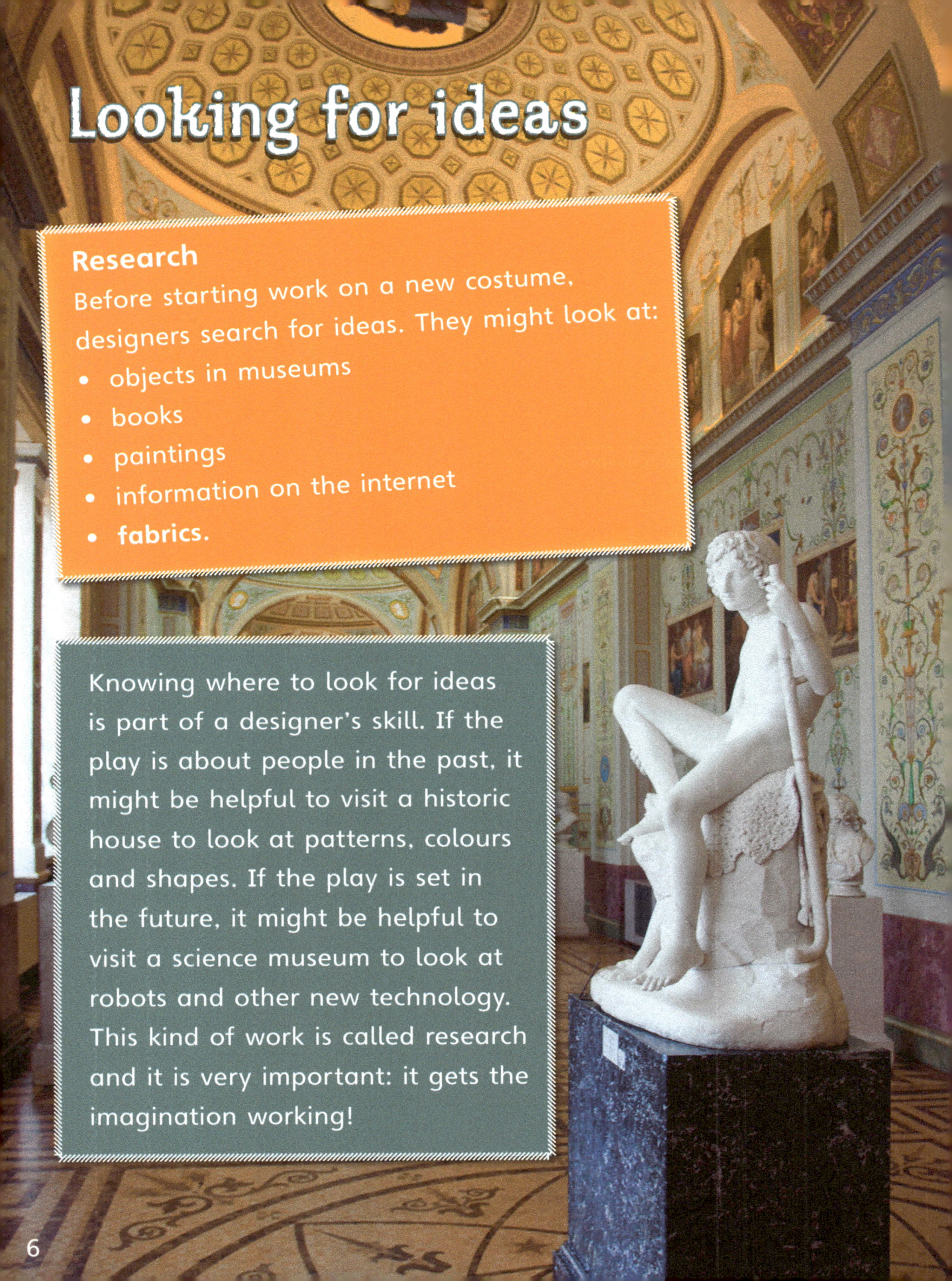

Research
Before starting work on a new costume, designers search for ideas. They might look at:
- objects in museums
- books
- paintings
- information on the internet
- **fabrics**.

Knowing where to look for ideas is part of a designer's skill. If the play is about people in the past, it might be helpful to visit a historic house to look at patterns, colours and shapes. If the play is set in the future, it might be helpful to visit a science museum to look at robots and other new technology. This kind of work is called research and it is very important: it gets the imagination working!

Historical rooms give designers ideas for fabrics, colours and styles.

A chandelier may inspire ideas for jewellery.

Curtains may inspire ideas for style details.

Furnishings may inspire ideas for fabric colour.

Try It!

Research costumes for a film set in ancient Rome. Where would you start looking for ideas?

Learning about the play | Research and preparation

Making a mood board

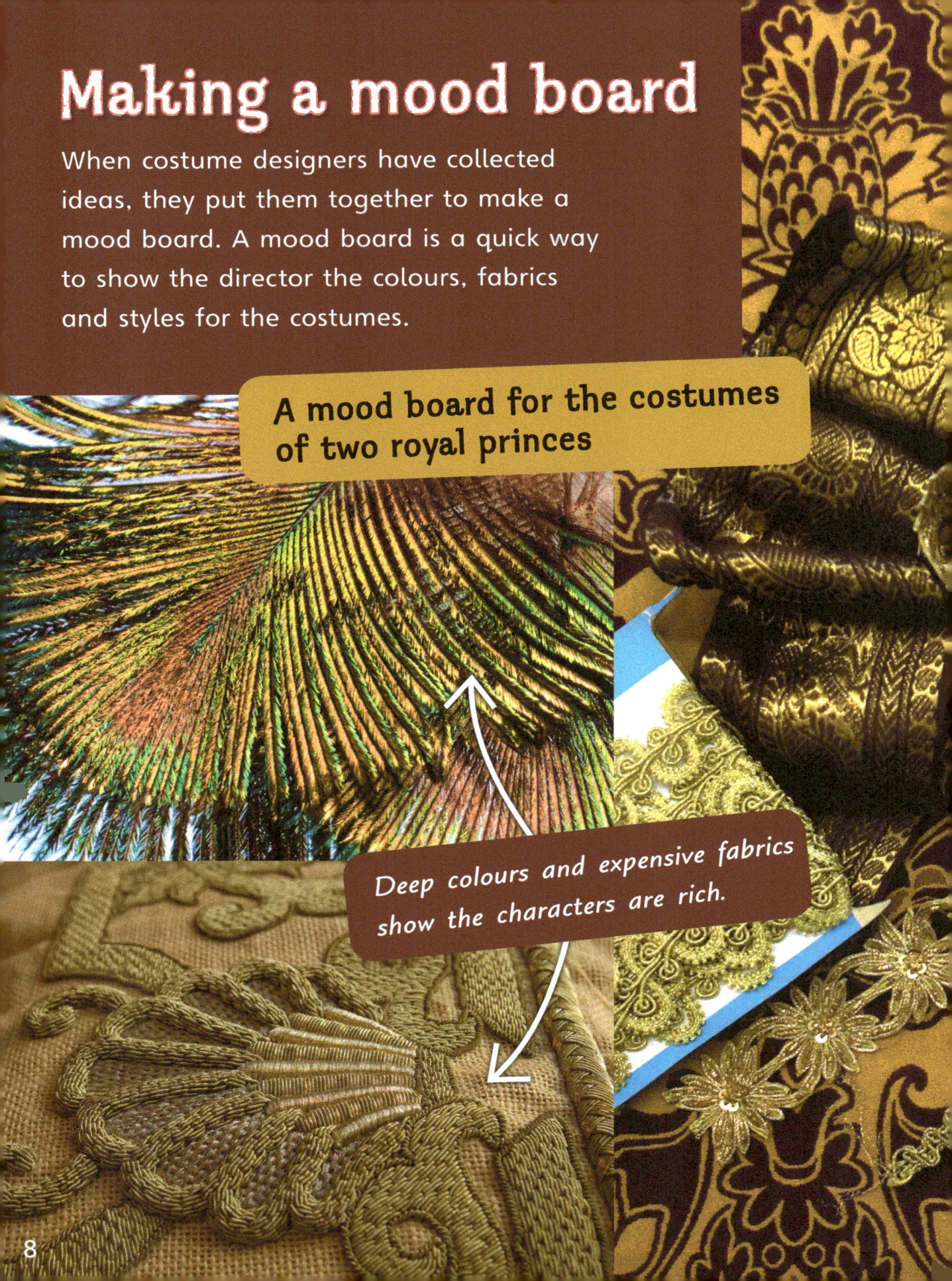

When costume designers have collected ideas, they put them together to make a mood board. A mood board is a quick way to show the director the colours, fabrics and styles for the costumes.

A mood board for the costumes of two royal princes

Deep colours and expensive fabrics show the characters are rich.

Big white lacy cuffs and collars show that the princes like extravagant, showy fashion.

Plenty of gold braid will make the princes stand out on stage.

Try It!

Make a mood board for the costume of a Snow King or Snow Queen. Collect ideas and experiment until you get a combination of colours, styles and textures that you are happy with.

Learning about the play | Research and preparation

Pencil to paper

Sketches

When the director is happy with the mood board, the designer begins to **sketch** the costume. Sketching is a way of trying out ideas.

- On TV and film, actors' faces are seen close up, so a sketch might show lots of interesting detail around the neck and shoulders. Which details will work best: beads, buttons, stitches or a collar?
- On stage, the actors are a long way from the audiences – so strong shapes and colours will work well.
- What about the back of the costume? That will need to be sketched too.

Designers work and re-work their ideas until they have a finished drawing. If the director likes the drawing, the costume goes ahead.

Did you know?

If a costume needs to show the passing of time, the designer will make two: one bright and new, the other dull and older looking.

Think about it!

When you start working on a costume, you need to know about the actor who will wear it. Is he tall or short, for example? What else would be useful to know?

The finished costume may be a bit different from the early sketch. Can you spot any differences?

Learning about the play | Research and preparation | Designing the costume

Finding the materials

Handing over

The designer gives the finished drawing to the costume supervisor. The supervisor will organise everything from now on – and there is a lot to do!

To do:
- Choose a costume maker
- Find a **prop** maker
- Find and buy all the materials – fabrics trimmings, buttons, etc
- Meet and measure the actors

Did you know?

Costumes are worn so many times that sometimes zips break, fabric tears or buttons drop off. The supervisor buys extra fabric and spares to do repairs.

The costume supervisor

"It's my job to bring the designer's drawing to life. I work with the costume maker, and check that the costumes are made perfectly and on time. You need to be organised for this job. You need a good eye, a good memory — and to know how to use a needle!"

Lots of measurements are taken from the actors to make sure the costumes fit properly.

It's important to put actors at ease by treating them with tact and care.

- A Chest
- B Waist
- C Hip
- D Outside leg
- E Inside leg
- F Neck
- G Sleeve
- H Head
- I Shoulders
- J Neck to waist
- K Neck to floor

Learning about the play | Research and preparation | Designing the costume | Planning the costume

Making the pattern

Paper and fabric

The costume supervisor gives the drawings, materials and measurements to the costume maker. It is the maker's job to produce a real **garment**. The first step is to make a pattern. A pattern is all the pieces in a costume drawn onto paper.

How to make and use a pattern

Step 1: Study the drawing and work out the pieces needed to make the costume — for example, the front, back and sleeves.
Step 2: Draw each piece on a big sheet of paper.
Step 3: Label and mark the pattern pieces, and cut them out.
Step 4: Pin the pattern pieces to the fabric.
Step 5: Cut around the pieces to get the fabric shapes.

The costume maker draws around a standard pattern piece. The paper pattern piece can then be adjusted to fit the actor.

Learning about the play | Research and preparation | Designing the costume | Planning the costume

14

The costume maker pins the paper pattern to the fabric, then carefully cuts round each piece.

All the paper patterns are clipped together, labelled and hung on a rail for future use.

Try It!
Place a T-shirt on a newspaper and draw around the body and sleeves separately. Turn the T-shirt over and do the same again. Cut out the pieces to make a pattern!

A test run

Testing the pattern
Some costumes are complicated and some of the fabrics they're made from are expensive. So that mistakes are not made, the costume maker may test out the pattern first, in a cheaper fabric.

Did you know?
Every costume is made for a particular actor but extra fabric is always left in the seams. Then the costume can be made larger if a bigger actor takes over the part.

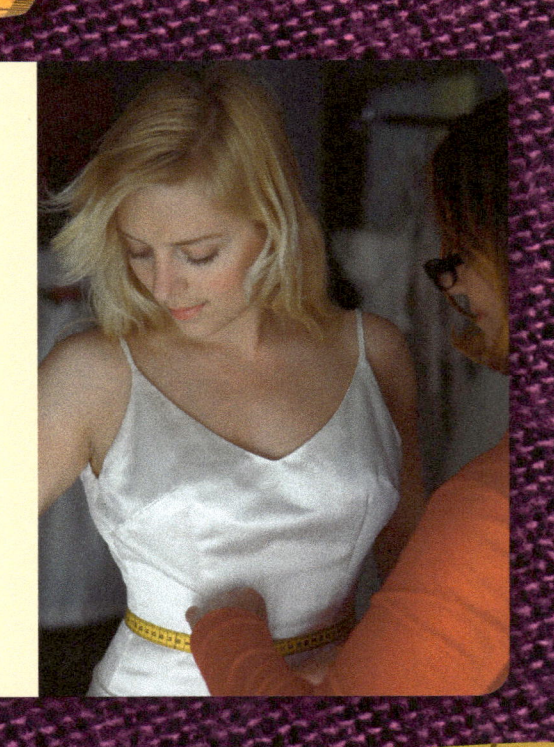

Learning about the play | Research and preparation | Designing the costume | Planning the costume

Trying on the costume

As the test garment takes shape, the maker puts it on a **dress form**. This makes it easier to improve the fit. Next, the actor is called for a fitting and tries the costume on. The supervisor and the costume maker look at the garment with their expert eyes. They alter and pin it to improve the fit. When they are happy with the test garment, it's time to use the proper fabric and start the real thing!

Costume makers often wear a pincushion on their wrists, so that pins aren't dropped or lost.

17

The sewing starts!

Keeping it simple

The costume maker cuts out the fabric and sews the pieces of the garment together. The maker uses long stitches that are easy to undo. No **trimmings** are added yet. Everything is kept very simple in case it has to be altered.

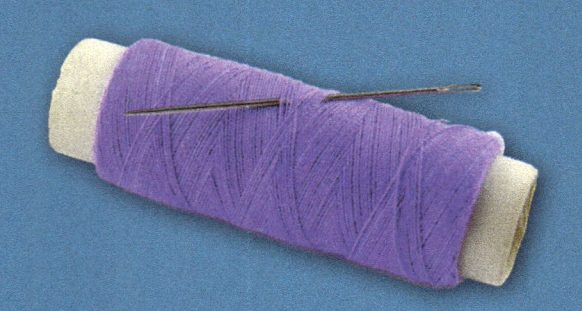

The sewing thread has to be a perfect match for the fabric, so the stitches are almost invisible.

The fitting

The actor is called for a costume fitting. The designer and the director are there too. They look at the costume and discuss any changes while the costume maker alters and pins it. The maker may need more fittings to get the costume exactly right.

Learning about the play

Did you know?

Actors sometimes play characters that are very large. They wear a fat-suit made of foam under their costumes.

An actor can get very warm wearing a fat-suit under a costume.

The costume maker

"I work in the costume workshop of a big theatre. I enjoy sewing and I have a good sense of colour and design. It's hard work - the hours can be long and sometimes there are panics! But I love working in a team and it's a great feeling when a costume turns out well."

Research and preparation | Designing the costume | Planning the costume | Making the costume

In the workshop

The dye room

Big theatres have special workshops, such as a dye room. The people here have many skills that help with the costumes. They can:

- mix dyes to get a perfect colour
- make a costume look much older than it is
- stain a costume with fake blood or fake sick
- make a spooky, grey fabric for a ghost.

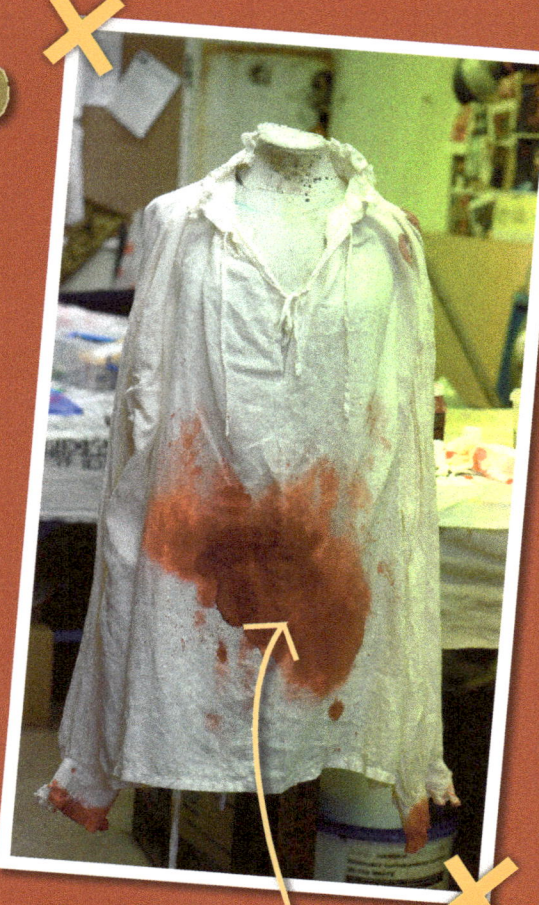

This shirt has been dyed to look as though the character wearing it has been injured.

Dyers mix and boil up dyes in large pans and vats. They wear gloves and aprons to protect themselves.

Learning about the play

The prop room

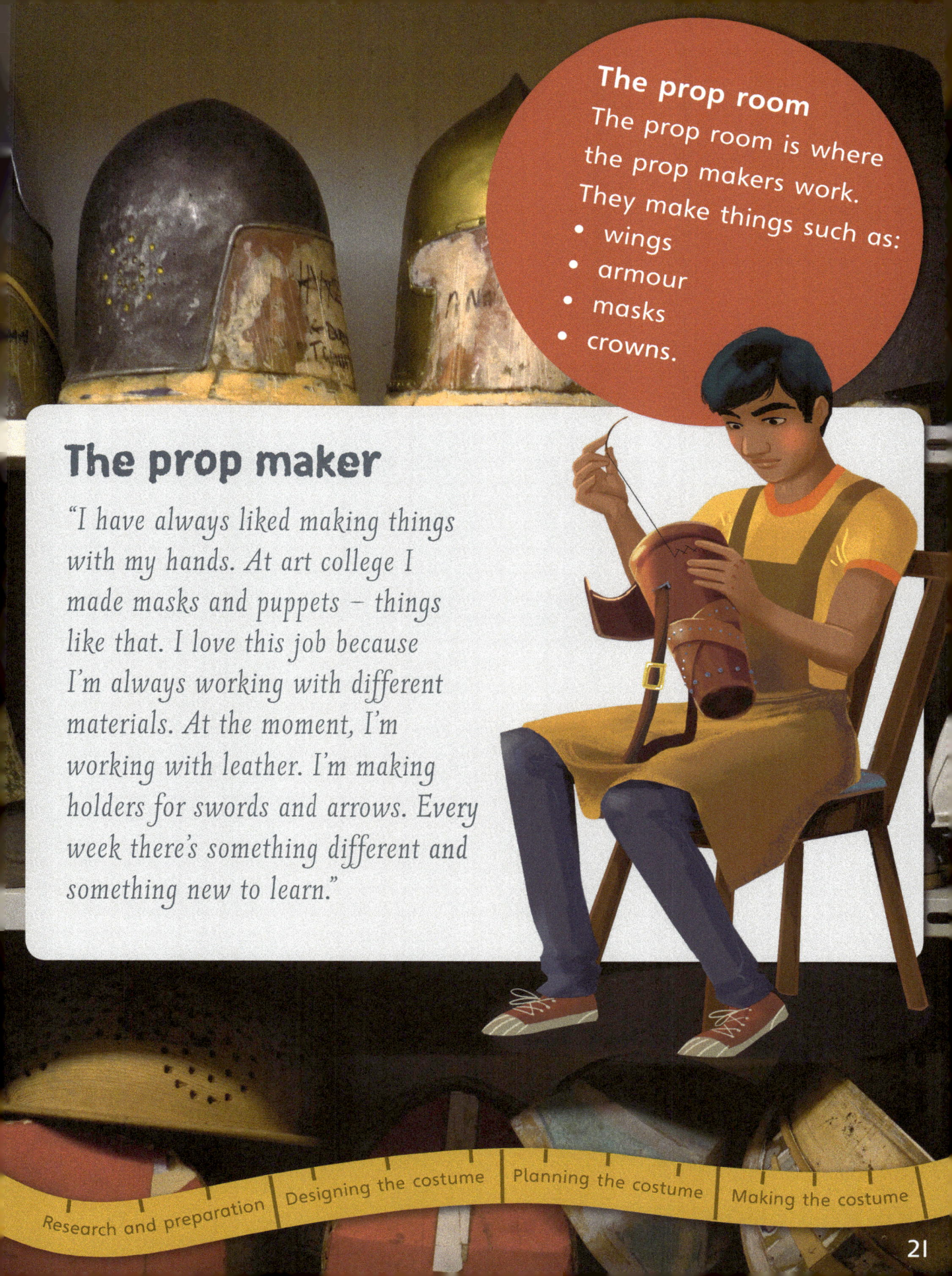

The prop room is where the prop makers work. They make things such as:
- wings
- armour
- masks
- crowns.

The prop maker

"I have always liked making things with my hands. At art college I made masks and puppets – things like that. I love this job because I'm always working with different materials. At the moment, I'm working with leather. I'm making holders for swords and arrows. Every week there's something different and something new to learn."

Research and preparation | Designing the costume | Planning the costume | Making the costume

The tricks of the trade

Costumes are not always what they seem. Costume makers know all sorts of tricks to make costumes quickly and cheaply. People sit so far from the stage that they are easily fooled.

This beautiful 'stitching' has been painted with a brush.

Learning about the play

Foil + Plexi + metal paint

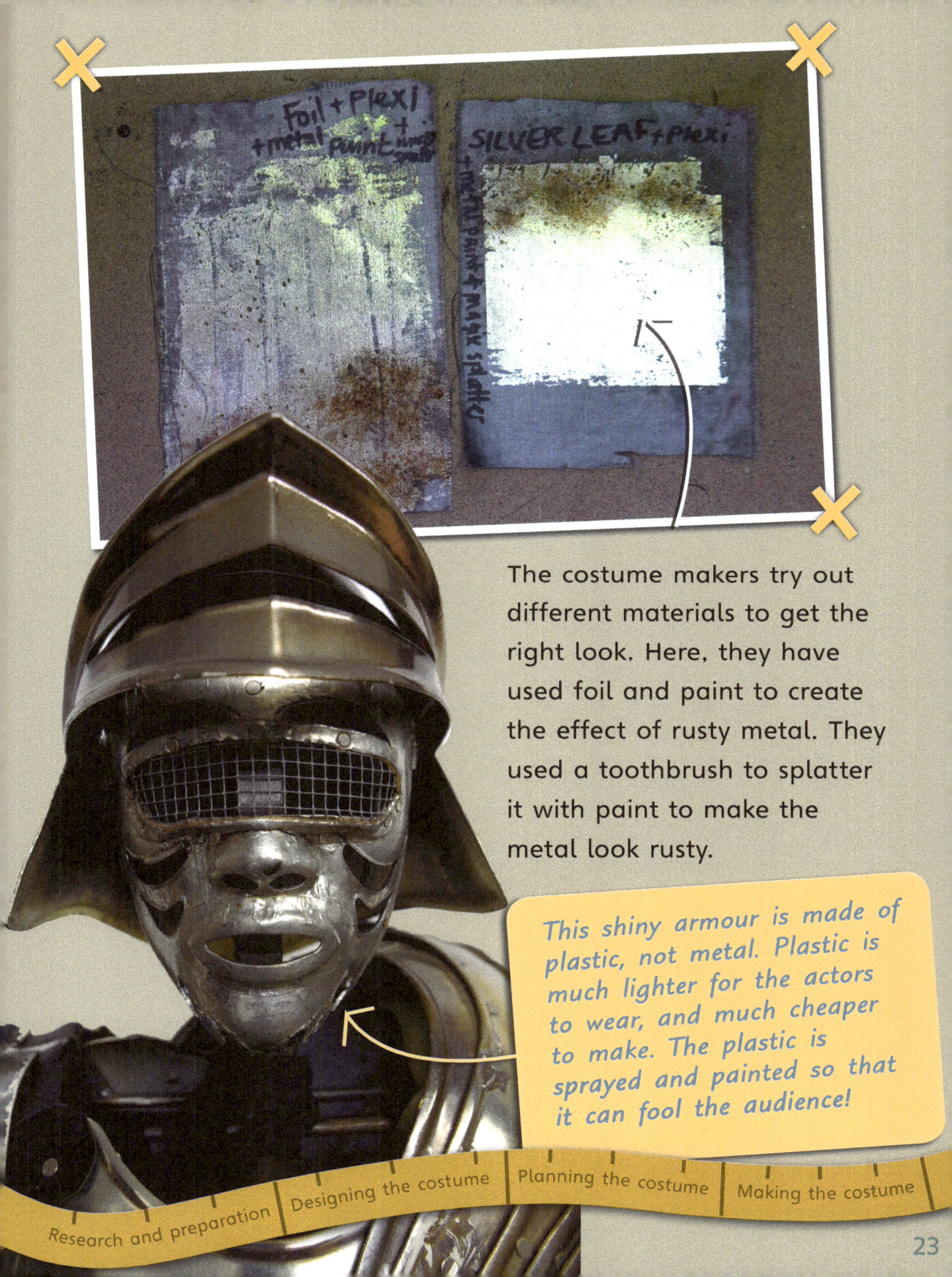

SILVER LEAF + Plexi

The costume makers try out different materials to get the right look. Here, they have used foil and paint to create the effect of rusty metal. They used a toothbrush to splatter it with paint to make the metal look rusty.

This shiny armour is made of plastic, not metal. Plastic is much lighter for the actors to wear, and much cheaper to make. The plastic is sprayed and painted so that it can fool the audience!

Research and preparation | Designing the costume | Planning the costume | Making the costume

23

The final touches

Getting it right
After every fitting, costume makers unpick their stitches and alter the garment to get a perfect fit. They might raise a pocket or lower the hem.

Dressing it up
Now it is time to 'dress' the costume. It may need bright brass buttons, flowers, or a trimming of fur and lace. The costume designer checks the garment and then chooses the extras to go with it, such as boots, socks, gloves, and a hat.

The final trimmings on a costume are sewn on by hand.

Fabric can be made to look old if it's scrubbed with a pumice stone.

Think about it!

How could you make a new costume look really old? Tricks include rubbing fabric with a cheese grater, and filling pockets with stones to make them sag! Can you think of anything else you could do?

Shoes bought for one play can be painted to match the costume in another.

Try It!

Design shoes or a hat for a pirate costume. What material, style and colour would you choose? What details could you add?

Designing the costume | Planning the costume | Making the costume | Adding the extras

To wardrobe

The finished costume

At last the costume is finished! The costume maker puts it on a hanger, and sends it to 'wardrobe'. The wardrobe team hang it on a rail with other costumes. They label each garment carefully with the name of the theatre, the play, the character and the actor. They add the **act** and scene numbers too.

In rehearsal

During the final **rehearsals** of the play, the actors wear the finished costumes. The costume designer, the supervisor and the costume maker are all on hand to dress the actors. They ask questions such as:

- How does your costume feel?
- Are the shoes slippery?
- Are there any problems?

Learning about the play | Research and preparation | Designing the costume | Planning the costume

Did you know?
The wardrobe team make a checklist of what each actor wears in every scene of the play. This is called the 'costume list'.

Example Costume List

Character: Wilma the Witch

Act 1
- Scene 1 – black tunic, stripy socks, black shoes, red T-shirt
- Scene 2 – as above, plus black cape, black hat, red gloves and broomstick
- Scene 3 – black pyjamas, red fluffy socks
- Scene 4 – black tunic, stripy socks, red boots, red hat

The Costume Bible
Every play has a book called the Costume Bible. It contains all the information about the costumes, such as the name of each fabric and where it was bought. This is a great help if anything needs buying later.

Making the costume | Adding the extras | To wardrobe

The opening night

In the dressing room

An hour before the actors go on stage, their costumes are taken to the dressing rooms. Dressers help the actors to get dressed and make any last minute changes. They also help with costume changes during the show. Hair and make-up artists arrive. Once the costume, wig and make-up are in place, the actor is ready for the stage.

Did you know?

Actors often have to change quickly between scenes. Quick-change costumes close with magnets because they don't get stuck like zips and are quieter than Velcro.

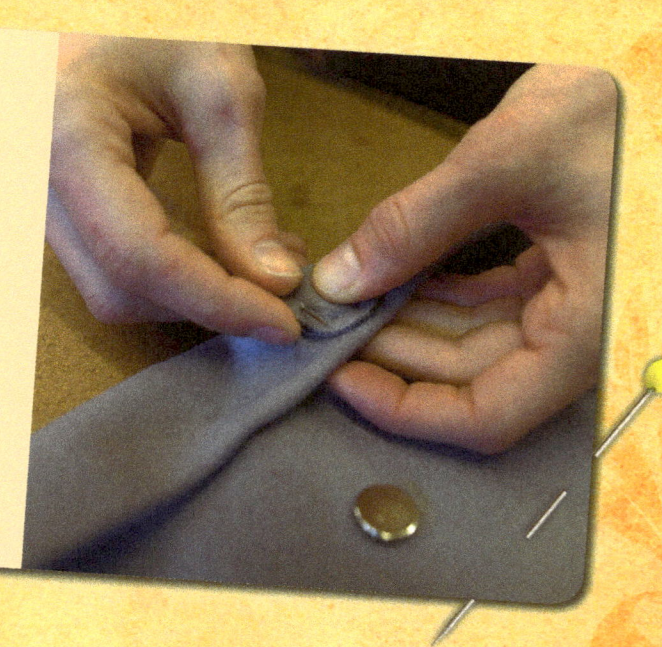

Dressers help actors with jewellery as well as clothes.

After the show

When the show has finished and the actors have gone home, the dressers gather up the costumes and return them to wardrobe. Many garments, such as shirts and socks, are washed and dried overnight. The dressers iron them the next day and make any repairs. They check the costumes and polish the shoes. Everything has to be ready for the next show.

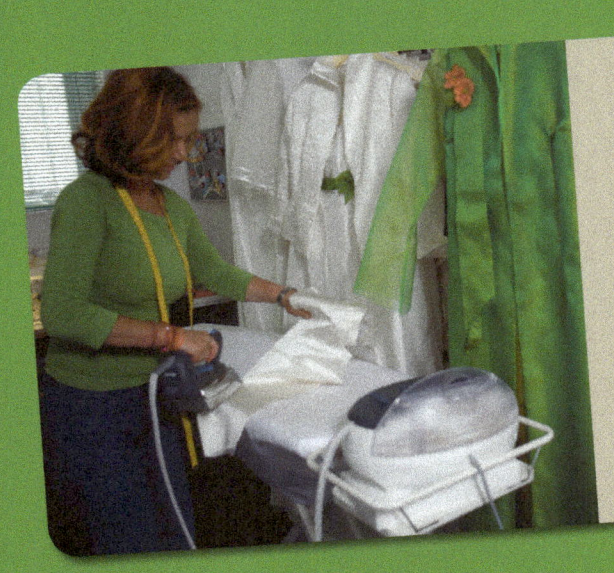

Did you know?

Dressers have to wash and iron the costumes carefully, because some fabrics are very delicate.

Making the costume | Adding the extras | To wardrobe | Opening night

Make a costume!

Choose a favourite character from a book or film and design a costume for him or her. Follow these steps:

1. Ask questions

Think hard about your character. Where do they live? What kind of things do they do? Are they rich or poor? Are they very active?

2. Research your costume

Think about colour, pattern and style. Think about materials and trimmings. Where could you go for good ideas?

3. Sort your ideas

Choose the ideas that you like most and use them to make a mood board.

4. Sketch your costume

What parts of your costume will people see? What details might it have? How will the actor put it on? Alter your sketch until you get it right. Add notes to explain your ideas.

5. Measuring up

Measure a person who could wear the costume. Look back at page 13 to see which measurements you need. Write them down.

6. Find your fabric!

Finally, look for the fabric and trimmings. Pin samples of them to your drawing.

Glossary

act (n) section of a play
director person in charge of the play
dress form model of a human body, used for fitting clothes
fabric cloth
garment piece of clothing
prop object used by actors in the play
rehearsal practice
scene section of an act
script words of the play
seam place where two pieces of cloth have been sewn together
sketch (v) draw quickly and roughly
trimming decorative material added to a costume

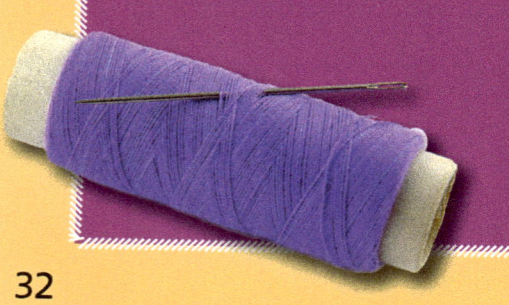

Index

actors 2, 10, 11, 13, 16, 17, 18, 26, 28
characters 2, 3, 4, 8, 26, 30
Costume Bible 27
costume designers 3, 4–11, 12, 18, 20, 24, 26
costume list 27
costume makers 12, 14–19, 22, 24, 26
costume supervisors 12–13, 14, 17, 26
directors 3, 10, 18
dressers 28, 29
fabrics 7, 8, 16, 27, 31
fat-suits 19
fittings 17, 18, 24
hiring costumes 2, 3
ideas 6–7, 8, 10, 30
measurements 13, 31
mood boards 8–9, 10, 30
padding 19
patterns 14–15, 16
prop makers 20, 21
quick-change costumes 28
rehearsals 26
repairs 12, 29
research 6, 7, 30
sewing 18
sketches 10, 11, 14, 31
test garments 16, 17
tricks of the trade 22–23, 25
trimmings 9, 10, 24, 31
wardrobe team 26, 27, 29
washing and ironing 29
workshops 19, 20